Fish and Seafood 48

Desserts 56

Recipes and Index 62

Thailand – the land of smiles

The very name of this beautiful country evokes a mass of different images in the minds of travellers and, indeed, anyone with an interest in Thailand. Some think of exotic temples, teak carvings, elephants and jungle. Others think of palm trees and long stretches of sun-drenched beaches. Surely many also think immediately of the exciting Thai cuisine. Thailand has a rich abundance of all of these to offer. From the beginning and throughout their whole stay there, newcomers to Thailand are always struck by the sheer friendliness and the smiling serenity of the people. This is why Thailand has become famous throughout the world as the land of smiles.

Translated literally, Thailand means the 'land of the free' and the country rightly bears this description for, although they have sometimes been conquered, the Thai people have never been subjugated. Thai kings have always been able to adapt important innovations and foreign imports into a Thai-friendly form.

Thailand lies at the cross-roads of various peoples, cultures and religions – halfway between India and China. It has been influenced by its neighbours, but has preserved its own unique culture and language, its traditional habits and customs. It has also retained its own unmistakable and utterly delicious cuisine. This, too, has been influenced by foreign imports made Thai-friendly. Chillies, for example, were, in fact, introduced by the Portuguese missionaries in the sixteenth century. Now, it is

Rice is the staple food in Thailand and is served with every meal.

difficult to believe that they were not indigenous, so typical are they of Thai cuisine and the very hot bird's eye or Thai chilli has become world famous.

Food in Thailand

If you walk through Bangkok at any time of day or night, you will immediately be aware of the innumerable food stalls. Some streets owe their entire character to them. There, you can witness all manner of foods being fried, grilled, stewed, poached and even flambéd – all within yards of each other. A bicycle or motorbike is quickly transformed into a mobile kitchen, able to fulfil its purpose wherever it is positioned.

You can lower yourself on to a rickety, three-legged wooden stool right in the middle of the bustling town or in one of the little side streets and just place your order as your mood takes you. If an extra dish from a neighbouring stall whets your appetite, you can order it without embarrassment. This is quite normal and gives no offence at all. Perhaps just when you want a dessert, a cart chances by from which melting ice cubes are

dripping and on which exotic, tropical fruits are offered for sale. Papayas, mangoes, rambutans or pineapples – just place your order and try them!

Another time let yourself be guided by the enticing smells that waft around you, for the air is filled with the aromas of curries, garlic, coriander and basil. Perhaps you can detect ginger or fish sauce, too. If you pass by someone cooking rice just when he is removing the lid, savour the unbelievably wonderful smell of the rice. Then you will understand why it is called *kao hom*, which means fragrant rice.

The eyes eat too

This saying is especially true of Thai food. We even know a group of fruit and vegetable carvers who, using special knives, create veritable works of art. A water melon becomes a carved green, white and red flower and carrots are turned into roses with leaves. Pumpkins are also carved into decorative serving dishes.

Even banana leaves are used to please the eye when they are cut into shape as a container for fresh

Thai
COOKING

A culinary journey through Thailand

Seductive aromas invite you to enjoy delicious Thai dishes. Exotic combinations of meat, seafood, rice, noodles, herbs and spices await you – prepared according to authentic recipes. In the following pages, you will learn all about lemon grass, curry pastes, coconut milk and Asian sauces.

Thai people always combine food with sanuk – fun. Lots of different dishes are served and many guests are invited to try them. Each guest seeks out his own particular favourite. Why not do the same and enjoy one of the best cuisines in the world?

AURA

CONTENTS

fruit or as parcels for a variety of tasty snacks. Why not follow their example and serve your fruit salad in a hollowed-out water melon or pineapple or in papaya halves. Your guests will love it!

Menu planning

Thais have no strict rules about meals – either concerning the time they eat or the content. Rice and soup are eaten, even in the morning, and there are no separate courses as in the West. All the dishes are served at the same time so that guests can choose from a wide range of different tastes and textures. Dishes are not eaten in any particular order.

Variety is what counts when putting a menu together: a mild dish is placed next to a spicy one, a grilled dish stands next to a steamed, soupy or crisp one. The ingredients, too, should be as varied as possible. A fish dish should accompany a meat dish, for example. The rule of thumb is the larger the number of dishes and the more varied the choice, the better. The absolute minimum is a soup and two main dishes.
A typical meal would include soup, curry, a fried dish, a steamed dish, perhaps a salad, one or two sauces or dips and, of course, a bowl of rice. However, do not be too rigid; vary and extend what you offer, add tasty morsels here and there and spoil your guests with variety.

All this adds *sanuk*, or fun, to the meal.

In Thailand, eating is regarded as one of life's greatest pleasures. Every meal is virtually a celebration and the more people gathered around the dining table, the happier everyone is. To be forced to eat alone is regarded as a very severe misfortune.

Equipment

No special equipment is required for cooking Thai meals. However, there are a few pieces that you might find helpful. A wok is ideal for stir-frying and can also be used for steaming, poaching and deep-frying. Its rounded base ensures that the food is quickly and evenly

Typical of Thailand – this imposing teak construction seems to be set in paradise.

cooked. A set of bamboo steamers is also a useful addition. These are very inexpensive and can be bought from most Chinese supermarkets. A pestle and mortar is the best method of grinding spices, but an electric coffee grinder kept specifically for the purpose will do as well.

If you eat rice every day, it is well worth buying an electric rice cooker, making sticky saucepans no more than a bad memory. It not only cooks the rice, it also keeps it warm. A wide range of types and sizes are available from many Chinese food stores.

Rice

The essential component of every meal is rice, a staple in the Thai diet. Thai farmers go to a lot of effort in order to grow rice, so it is regarded with some respect. It must not be wasted or thrown away – the very last grain must be eaten. In poorer areas, rice is often eaten without any accompanying dishes, except, perhaps, for some fish sauce to season it.

There are several types of rice, but one of the most popular in Thailand is fragrant rice, sometimes called jasmine rice, which is always cooked without the addition of any salt.

In the north and east of the country, people prefer glutinous or sticky rice. It is softened by soaking overnight so that the grains stick together tightly when it is cooked. It can then be eaten with the fingers or chopsticks.

The colourful and bustling floating markets are among the most fascinating places to visit in Thailand.

Boiled rice

KAO SUAY

Easy to prepare

Serves 4
250 g/9 oz fragrant Thai rice
about 750 ml/1¼ pints water

Approximately per portion:
910 kj/220 kcal • 5 g protein
1 g fat • 46 g carbohydrate

● Approximate preparation
   time: 20 minutes

---

1. Rinse the rice under cold running water and put into a large saucepan. Add sufficient water to cover the rice by 2 cm/¾ inch.

2. Cover and bring to the boil. Remove the lid and lower the heat. When the rice is gently simmering, replace the lid and simmer over a low heat for about 20 minutes, until the rice is tender and has absorbed the water.

Tip

For fried rice dishes, remove the lid and allow the rice to cool completely before frying.

Special ingredients

Oyster Sauce
(Nam manhoy)
This thick, spicy sauce is available from many supermarkets and Asian stores. It is made from oyster extract and soy sauce and can be kept for several months in the refrigerator.

Bamboo shoots
Canned bamboo shoots are available from most supermarkets and fresh bamboo shoots can sometimes be obtained from Asian shops. The fresh shoots are fairly time-consuming to prepare and take a long time to cook. Canned shoots are usually thinly sliced, but whole shoots, which have a better flavour, are available. Rinse canned bamboo shoots thoroughly before use and use in meat and vegetable soup.

Basil
Two types of basil are used in this book: sweet basil (bai horapa) and Thai or Holy basil (bai grapao). When recipes refer to Thai basil, the fresh leaves of bai grapao should be used. It has a slightly hot taste and is usually available from Asian shops. Bai horapa has a stronger flavour than western basil and tastes a little like aniseed.

Wood ear mushrooms
Not strictly speaking mushrooms, this fungus can be bought dried in Chinese and Asian stores. Wood ears need to be softened by soaking them in hot water for about 20 minutes. Then remove the hard stems if necessary.

Chillies
Fresh and dried chillies are available in a huge variety of sizes, colours and degrees of spiciness. As a general rule, the smaller they are, the hotter. If you prefer a milder taste, remove the seeds before cooking. Thai chillies, also known as bird's eye chillies, may be red or green. They are small and extremely hot.

Curry pastes
Many of the following recipes recommend the use of various curry pastes. Thai cooks usually make their own, but ready-made pastes are available from some supermarkets and Asian stores. They are of excellent quality and considerably simplify the preparation of Thai dishes. Curry pastes keep for several months in the refrigerator. The following pastes are used in the recipes in this book:
● red curry paste
   (gang ped dang)
● green curry paste
   (gang kiau wan)
● Panang curry paste
   (gang Panang)
● Mussaman curry paste
   (gang Mussaman)
● roasted curry paste
   (nam prik pao).

Fish sauce
(Nam pla)
This is a thin, strong-flavoured, salty sauce made from fermented anchovies.

Spring roll skins
These can be bought frozen or dried in Asian shops. Thaw frozen skins before using. You can substitute wafer-thin pancakes.

Galangal

(Kha)

Also called galingale or 'Siamese ginger', the fresh root, which belongs to the same family as ginger, is somewhat larger and lighter in colour than root ginger and has pink tips. It tastes quite lemony and is used in the same way as fresh root ginger. It is available from Asian shops and is easy to freeze. Instead of galangal, you can use Laos powder (follow the instructions on the packet) or substitute fresh root ginger.

Ginger

Peel and finely slice, chop or grate the fresh root. Ground ginger is never used in Thai cooking and does not have the same flavour. When buying, choose plump roots with smooth skin. The roots can be preserved for some time if they are kept covered in sand. Ginger is not so widely used in Thai cooking as galangal.

Coconut milk

This is not the same as the 'milk' from a fresh coconut. Canned, dried and compressed blocks of coconut milk are available from Asian shops. Alternatively, you can make it yourself. Pour 250 ml/ 8 fl oz boiling water over 250 g/ 9 oz grated coconut flesh and set aside for about 15 minutes. Then knead the mixture well and strain through clean muslin. Stand the milk in the refrigerator until a thick coconut cream forms.

Coriander

An essential herb for Thai cooking, fresh coriander is widely available in supermarkets and Asian shops. You can also grow it easily from seed. Asian shops often sell fresh coriander with the roots still on, as these are often used in cooking. If necessary, parsley roots can be used as a substitute, but the flavour of the dish will no longer be typically Thai.

Palm sugar

This hard, brown sugar is obtained from the sap of the coconut palm and is available from Asian stores. It has a strong flavour. Soft brown sugar is a satisfactory substitute.

Rice noodles

These flat white noodles are made from ground rice. They come in a variety of widths and both fresh and dried noodles are available from Asian stores.

Beansprouts

Fresh beansprouts are available from most supermarkets. You can also sprout mung beans yourself. When buying, choose firm, crisp beansprouts that do not have a strong smell.

Soy sauce

Made from fermented soy beans, the sauce can be both light and dark. Both kinds are used in the recipes in this book. When shopping, make sure you do not buy sweetened soy sauce or Japanese soy sauce, which is not so strong tasting.

Tapioca meal

A starch meal made from the tapioca tuber.

Kaffir lime leaves

(Makrut)

These may be used finely chopped or cooked whole in the dish and then removed before serving. They are very pungent with a strong lime flavour. Available from Asian stores, kaffir lime leaves are characteristic of Thai cuisine. They freeze well.

Lemon grass

Use only the lower 12 cm/5 inches of this long-stalked, fibrous herb. Press the lemon grass flat before using to release the aroma. Remove the stalks from the dish before serving as they are very woody.

Chinese chives

A member of the onion family, these are also known as garlic chives. They have a unique flavour that resembles a combination of onion and garlic. The stems may be used with or without their flowers. They are available from Asian food stores and some supermarkets. They will keep for two or three days in the salad drawer of the refrigerator.

The most important ingredients:
1. Bamboo shoots 2. Ginger 3. Light soy sauce 4. Fish sauce 5. Oyster sauce 6. Rice noodles 7. Panang curry paste 8. Red curry paste 9. Galangal 10. Roasted curry paste 11. Mussaman curry paste 12. Green curry paste 13. Coconut milk 14. Palm sugar 15. Tapioca meal 16. Beansprouts 17. Wood ear mushrooms 18. Basil 19. Spring roll skins 20. Basil 21. Coriander 22. Kaffir lime leaves 23. Lemon grass 24. Chillies

Chilli sauce with coriander

NAM PLA PRIK

Easy to prepare

Serves 4
4 fresh chillies
2 garlic cloves
45 ml/3 tablespoons fish sauce
30 ml/2 tablespoons lemon juice
I sprig fresh coriander

Approximately per portion:
45 kj/10 kcal
I g protein
0 g fat
2 g carbohydrate

- Approximate preparation
  time: 15 minutes

I. Seed the chillies and pound the flesh in mortar with a pestle or finely chop.

2. Finely chop the garlic and mix together with the chillies, fish sauce and lemon juice.

3. Finely chop the stalk and leaves of the fresh coriander and add to the chilli sauce.

Variation
You can also add a few thinly sliced shallots or a thinly sliced red onion to the sauce.

Sweet-and-sour spicy sauce

NAM JIM PRIAU WAN

Famous recipe

Serves 4
½ red pepper
2 fresh red chillies
I garlic clove
250 ml/8 fl oz water
75 ml/5 tablespoons rice wine or
    rice vinegar
150 ml/10 tablespoons sugar

Approximately per portion:
620 kj/150 kcal
0 g protein
0 g fat
36 g carbohydrate

- Approximate preparation
  time: 45 minutes

I. Core, seed and roughly chop the red pepper. Seed and roughly chop the chillies.

2. Pound the red pepper, chillies and garlic together in a mortar with a pestle. Transfer the mixture to a small saucepan.

3. Add the water, rice wine or rice vinegar and sugar and bring to the boil, stirring constantly.

4. Simmer, uncovered, over a medium heat for 30 minutes until thickened. Serve hot or cold.

Variation
You can also add wafer-thin slices of cucumber or ground peanuts to the sauce.

Tip

Sweet-and-sour spicy sauce can be stored for up to 4 weeks in a screw-top jar in the refrigerator.

Simple chilli sauce

NAM JIM PRIKBON

Easy to make

Serves 4
2 garlic cloves
60 ml/4 tablespoons fish sauce
30 ml/2 tablespoons lemon juice
15 ml/ I tablespoon palm sugar or
    soft brown sugar
15 ml/I tablespoon chilli powder

Approximately per portion:
100 kj/25 kcal
I g protein
0 g fat
6 g carbohydrate

- Approximate preparation
  time: 10 minutes

I. Pound the garlic in a mortar with a pestle, then transfer to a small serving bowl.

2. Add the fish sauce, lemon juice, sugar and chilli powder. Stir until the sugar has dissolved.

Above: Sweet-and-sour spicy sauce
Centre: Simple chilli sauce
Below: Chilli sauce with coriander

Soup with wonton pouches

GAU NAM

Easy to make

Serves 4
4 garlic cloves
115 g/4 oz of minced pork
freshly ground black pepper
60 ml/4 tablespoons fish sauce
20 wonton wrappers
15 ml/1 tablespoon vegetable oil
500 ml/17 fl oz water
30 ml/2 tablespoons beef
*   stock granules*
fresh coriander, to garnish

Approximately per portion:
810 kj/190 kcal
7 g protein
14 g fat
10 g carbohydrate

● Approximate preparation
  time: 30 minutes

---

1. Finely chop 1 garlic clove. Season the minced pork well with pepper, then mix in the garlic and 15 ml/1 tablespoon of the fish sauce.

2. Put 5 ml/1 teaspoon of the meat into the centre each of the wonton wrappers. Gather together the corners of each wonton wrapper to make a pouch, then lightly press together in the middle to seal.

3. Finely chop the remaining garlic. Heat the oil in a small frying pan and fry the garlic over a medium heat until golden. Remove the pan from the heat and set aside.

4. Bring the water to the boil in a saucepan. Stir in the stock granules and the remaining fish sauce. Lower the heat. Place the wonton pouches carefully into the simmering broth and cook for about 1 minute, or until cooked through.

5. Transfer the soup to serving bowls, garnish with coriander leaves and the garlic and serve.

Chicken soup with lemon grass

TOM KA GAI

Famous recipe

Serves 4
2 stalks lemon grass
5 cm/2 inch piece fresh galangal
3 kaffir lime leaves
250 g/9 oz oyster mushrooms
2 medium-sized tomatoes
3 fresh Thai chillies
500 g/1¼ lb boneless chicken
*   breasts, skinned*
400 ml/14 fl oz coconut milk
750 ml/1¼ pints water
60 ml/4 tablespoons lemon juice
60 ml/4 tablespoons fish sauce
fresh coriander, to garnish

Approximately per portion:
720 kj/170 kcal
31 g protein
2 g fat
6 g carbohydrate

● Approximate preparation
  time: 30 minutes

---

1. Cut the lemon grass into 3 cm/1¼ inch pieces. Thinly slice the galangal. Cut the kaffir lime leaves into quarters.

2. Tear the mushrooms into bite-size pieces. Cut the tomatoes into quarters. Thinly slice the chillies into rings. Cut the chicken breasts into thin strips approximately 1 cm/½ inch wide and 4 cm/1½ inches long.

3. Heat the coconut milk in a small saucepan. Add the lemon grass, kaffir lime leaves and galangal. Boil the coconut milk over a medium heat for about 2 minutes.

4. Add the water and bring back to the boil. Add the chicken, mushrooms and tomatoes and simmer for a further 5 minutes.

5. Divide the chillies, lemon juice and fish sauce between 4 individual soup bowls. Remove the lemon grass and galangal from the soup and discard. Pour the hot soup into the bowls, garnish with the coriander and serve.

Variation
This fiery soup also tastes good with the addition of cod or monkfish filets.

Tip

Lemon grass is used only for flavouring and should never be eaten with the dish, as it is too woody. Galangal may also be removed from cooked dishes before serving.

Above: Chicken soup with lemon grass
Below: Soup with wonton pouches

Cellophane noodle soup with minced meat

GANG DUT WUNSEN

Quick and cheap

Serves 4
115 g/4 oz cellophane noodles
2 sprigs fresh coriander, with roots
5 pak choi leaves
3 garlic cloves
2.5 ml/½ teaspoon peppercorns
2.5 ml/½ teaspoon salt
250 g/9 oz mixed minced meat
freshly ground black pepper
1 litre/1¾ pints water
30 ml/2 tablespoons beef
*   stock granules*
45 ml/3 tablespoons fish sauce

Approximately per portion:
910 kj/220 kcal
14 g protein
13 g fat
13 g carbohydrate

● Approximate preparation
   time: 20 minutes

---

1. Soak the noodles in warm water for about 10 minutes, until softened. Drain and chop.

2. Cut off and reserve the coriander roots. Finely chop the leaves. Shred the pak choi leaves. Put the garlic, coriander roots, peppercorns and salt in a mortar and pound together with a pestle.

3. Season the minced meat with a little more salt and pepper, if liked. Bring the water to the boil in a medium saucepan. Stir in the stock granules and the garlic and coriander paste and bring back to the boil. Stir in the minced meat and simmer for about 2 minutes over a medium heat, until cooked.

4. Stir in the pak choi, noodles and fish sauce and simmer for a further 1 minute. Adjust the seasoning, if necessary. Transfer to 4 individual soup bowls, garnish with the chopped coriander and serve.

Fiery prawn soup

TOM YAM GUNG

Rather expensive

Serves 4
500 g/1¼ lb raw prawns
500 ml/17 fl oz water
1 sprig fresh coriander with roots
2.5 ml/½ teaspoon black
*   peppercorns*
300 g/11 oz mushrooms
2 lemon grass stems
3 kaffir lime leaves
4–5 cm/1½–2 inch piece
*   fresh galangal*
4 fresh Thai chillies
45 ml/3 tablespoons lemon juice
45 ml/3 tablespoons fish sauce

Approximately per portion:
540 kj/130 kcal
26 g protein
2 g fat
2 g carbohydrate

● Approximate preparation
   time: 45 minutes

---

1. Peel and devein the prawns, leaving the tails intact. Remove and reserve the heads and reserve the shells to make the stock.

2. Put the prawn heads and shells and the water in a medium saucepan and bring to the boil. Lower the heat and simmer. Cut off and reserve the coriander roots. Reserve the leaves. Pound together the coriander roots and the peppercorns in a mortar with a pestle. Add the mixture to the pan and simmer over a medium heat for about 5 minutes. Remove from the heat, strain through a fine sieve and reserve.

3. Cut the mushrooms in half. Cut the lemon grass into 3 cm/1¼ inch pieces and crush in a mortar with a pestle. Cut the kaffir lime leaves into quarters. Thinly slice the galangal.

4. Seed and slice the chillies into rings. Put them in a tureen together with the lemon juice and fish sauce.

5. Put the reserved prawn stock, lemon grass, kaffir lime leaves and the galangal in a medium saucepan and bring to the boil. Lower the heat and simmer for about 2 minutes. Add the prawns and mushrooms and simmer for a further 3 minutes over a medium heat. Remove the lemon grass, kaffir lime leaves and galangal from the soup.

6. Add the soup to the chilli mixture in the tureen, garnish with the coriander leaves and serve.

Above: Fiery prawn soup
Below: Cellophane noodle soup with minced meat

Pork satay with peanut sauce

MU SATE

Rather time-consuming

Thais love these delicious skewers of spicy marinated meat, which originally came from Indonesia. They can be served as a starter, a snack or as one of a selection of main-course dishes.

Serves 4
500 g/1¼ lb pork escalopes
150 g/5 oz roasted peanuts
2 cm/¾ inch piece fresh galangal
1 piece lemon grass
5 ml/1 teaspoon coriander seeds
5 ml/1 teaspoon cumin seeds
7.5 ml/1½ teaspoons salt
2.5 ml/½ teaspoon black pepper
90 g/3½ oz sugar
15 ml/1 tablespoon curry powder
400 ml/14 fl oz coconut milk
45 ml/3 tablespoons vegetable oil
30 ml/2 tablespoons red curry paste
45 ml/3 tablespoons palm sugar or
*   soft brown sugar*
about 250 ml/8 fl oz Chinese
*   rice wine*
1 cucumber
5 shallots
1 fresh red chilli
120 ml/4 fl oz water

Approximately per portion:
2,700 kj/640 kcal
37 g protein
37 g fat
43 g carbohydrate

● Approximate preparation
  time: 2 hours (1 hour
  marinating time)

1. Cut the pork escalopes into strips about 10 cm/4 inches long and 3 cm/1¼ inches wide and place in a large shallow dish. Pound the peanuts in a mortar with a pestle and set aside.

2. Finely chop the galangal. Thinly slice the lemon grass. Pound together the galangal, lemon grass, coriander and cumin seeds in a mortar with a pestle. Sprinkle this over the pork. Mix together 2.5 ml/½ teaspoon of salt, the pepper, 15 ml/1 tablespoon of the sugar, the curry powder and 45 ml/3 tablespoons of thick coconut milk. Pour over the pork strips.

3. Set the pork aside in the refrigerator to marinate for at least 1 hour. Remove the pork from the marinade and thread on to wooden or bamboo skewers in concertina fashion.

4. Heat the oil in a saucepan. Add the curry paste and stir-fry for 1 minute. Stir in the remaining coconut milk, bring to the boil and cook for 1 minute. Add the peanuts, palm or soft brown sugar, the remaining salt and 45 ml/3 tablespoons of the rice wine. Lower the heat and simmer for about 15 minutes, until thick. Transfer to a serving bowl.

5. Peel the cucumber, cut lengthways into quarters and then into wafer-thin slices. Thinly slice the shallots. Seed the chilli and cut the flesh into thin rings.

Variation
You can also make satays with steak or chicken breasts and serve with warm peanut sauce.

Tip

To prevent wooden or bamboo skewers from charring during cooking, soak them in a bowl of cold water before threading on the meat.

6. Bring the water to the boil. Add the remaining rice wine, the remaining sugar and a pinch of salt, if liked, and cook, stirring constantly, for about 1 minute, until the sugar has dissolved completely. Remove from the heat and set aside to cool.

7. Shortly before serving, mix together the cucumber, shallots and the cooled sugar sauce. Adjust the seasoning if necessary.

8. Cook the pork skewers on a barbecue, a preheated grill or in a preheated oven at 200°/400°F/ Gas 6 for 5–8 minutes, brushing with the marinade occasionally, until they are golden brown and the meat is cooked through. Serve immediately with the slightly warm peanut sauce.

Minced beef squares

KANOMPAN NA MU

Easy and quick to make

Serves 4
6 slices day-old white bread
1 garlic clove
200 g/7 oz minced beef
1 egg
15 ml/1 tablespoon dark
    soy sauce
salt
freshly ground black pepper
vegetable oil, for deep-frying
Sweet-and-sour spicy sauce, to serve

Approximately per portion:
2,400 kj/570 kcal
14 g protein
50 g fat
15 g carbohydrate
● Approximate preparation time: 20 minutes

1. Remove the crusts from the bread, then cut the slices into quarters. Finely chop the garlic.

2. Mix together the minced beef, egg, garlic and soy sauce and season to taste with salt and pepper. Spread each square of bread with about 5 ml/1 teaspoon of the mixture.

3. Heat the oil in a deep-fat fryer or wok. Fry the squares in batches for about 3 minutes. Drain on kitchen paper and keep warm while you cook the remaining batches. Serve with Sweet-and-sour spicy sauce (recipe on page 10).

Tip

Always use day-old bread, as this absorbs less oil.

Spring rolls

PBO-PBIA

For guests

Spring rolls are a very popular snack in Thailand. Making the spring roll skins is rather complicated, so it is better to use ready-made spring roll skins.

Serves 5
20 spring roll skins
90 g/3½ oz cellophane noodles
90 g/3½ oz white cabbage
50 g/2 oz carrots
2 garlic cloves
30 ml/2 tablespoons sunflower oil
250 g/9 oz minced beef or pork
30 ml/2 tablespoons fish sauce
15 ml/1 tablespoon sugar
30 ml/2 tablespoons oyster sauce
1 egg white
vegetable oil, for deep-frying
Sweet-and-sour spicy sauce, to serve

Approximately per portion:
1,900 kj/450 kcal
12 g protein
37 g fat
16 g carbohydrate
● Approximate preparation time: 1 hour

1. Thaw the spring roll skins, if frozen. Soak the spring roll skins, if dried. Soak the cellophane noodles in warm water for about

---

10 minutes. Drain thoroughly, then cut into small pieces with scissors.

2. Shred the white cabbage and cut the carrots into matchstick strips. Crush the garlic.

3. Heat the sunflower oil in a frying pan. Stir-fry the garlic for 1 minute. Add the minced meat and stir-fry over a high heat for about 2 minutes. Add the cabbage, carrots and noodles. Stir in the fish sauce, sugar and oyster sauce and continue to stir-fry for about 3 minutes. Remove the pan from the heat and set aside to cool.

4. Place 10 ml/2 teaspoons of the cooled filling on the middle of each spring roll skin. Fold one corner of each wrapper over the filling, and roll tightly, wrapping in the edges. Brush the edge with egg white and press to seal.

5. Heat the oil in a deep-fryer or wok. It will be hot enough when a wooden spoon placed in it causes little bubbles to rise. Fry the spring rolls, in batches if necessary, in the hot oil for about 3 minutes, until they are golden. Drain on kitchen paper and serve with Sweet-and-sour spicy sauce (recipe on page 10).

Tip

The uncooked spring rolls are ideal for freezing. However, do not re-freeze thawed, frozen spring roll skins.

Right: Minced beef squares
Left: Spring rolls

Beef-and-sweetcorn mini burgers

TOD MAN KAO POD

Easy to make

Serves 4
340 g/11½ oz can sweetcorn kernels
2 garlic cloves
115 g/4 oz minced beef
5 ml/1 teaspoon salt
2.5 ml/½ teaspoon pepper
1 egg yolk
5 ml/1 teaspoon sugar
30 ml/2 tablespoons flour
50–75 g/2–3 oz fresh
    white breadcrumbs
vegetable oil, for deep-frying
Sweet-and-sour spicy sauce, to serve

Approximately per portion:
2,300 kj/550 kcal
9 g protein
45 g fat
24 g carbohydrate

● Approximate preparation
  time: 40 minutes

---

1. Drain the sweetcorn thoroughly. Crush the garlic.

2. Mix together the minced beef, salt, pepper, garlic, egg yolk, sugar, flour and sweetcorn.

3. Spread the breadcrumbs on a large plate. Using the palms of your hands, shape 15 ml/1 tablespoon of the mixture into a burger about 4 cm/1½ inches in diameter. Turn the burger in the breadcrumbs to coat and gently press them in.

4. Heat the oil in deep-fat fryer or wok. The oil will be hot enough when a wooden spoon placed in it causes small bubbles to rise. Fry the burgers in the oil for about 3 minutes, then drain on kitchen paper. Serve with Sweet-and-sour spicy sauce (recipe on page 10).

Tip

You can vary the Sweet-and-sour spicy sauce by adding ground peanuts and thinly sliced, peeled cucumber.

Baked meatballs

MU SARONG

Sophisticated and inexpensive

Serves 4
1 garlic clove
250 g/9 oz minced pork
2.5 ml/½ teaspoon pepper
30 ml/2 tablespoons fish sauce
15 ml/1 tablespoon dark soy sauce
90 g/3½ oz flour
1 egg
2.5 ml/½ teaspoon salt
15–30 ml/1–2 tablespoons water
1 egg white
vegetable oil, for brushing and deep-frying
Simple chilli sauce, to serve

Approximately per portion:
2,100 kj/500 kcal
17 g protein
39 g fat
21 g carbohydrate

● Approximate preparation
  time: 1 hour

---

1. Preheat the oven to 200°C/400°F/Gas 6. Line a baking sheet with aluminium foil and brush with a little vegetable oil.

2. Finely chop the garlic. Mix together the minced pork, garlic, pepper, fish sauce and soy sauce and knead well. Using the palms of your hands, shape the mixture into balls of about 3 cm/1¼ inches in diameter and arrange on the baking sheet.

3. Bake the meatballs in the oven for about 15 minutes. Remove from the oven and set aside to cool slightly.

4. Meanwhile, mix together the flour, egg, salt and sufficient water to make a smooth, elastic dough. Roll out the dough on a lightly floured surface until it is very thin. Cut the dough into 3 mm/⅛ inch wide strips.

5. Brush 1 end of a dough strip with egg white and wrap it tightly around a meatball. Brush the other end with egg white and press to seal. Wrap all the meatballs with dough strips in the same way.

6. Heat the oil in a deep-fryer or wok. Fry the meatballs, in batches if necessary, for about 3 minutes, until golden brown. Drain on kitchen paper. Serve immediately with Simple chilli sauce (recipe on page 10).

Above: Baked meatballs
Below: Beef-and-sweetcorn mini burgers

Squid salad

YAM PLA MUK

Rather time-consuming

Serves 4
1 white onion
1 red onion
5 fresh chillies
1 sprig fresh coriander, with roots
3 garlic cloves
45 ml/3 tablespoons fish sauce
45 ml/3 tablespoons lemon juice
5 ml/1 teaspoon sugar
500 g/1¼ lb squid, cleaned
lettuce leaves, to serve

Approximately per portion:
460 kj/110 kcal
20 g protein
1 g fat
5 g carbohydrate

● Approximate preparation
time: 1 hour

---

1. Thinly slice the onions and push out into rings. Halve and seed the chillies. Cut off and reserve the coriander root. Finely chop the stalk and leaves.

2. Pound together the coriander root, chilli and garlic in a mortar with a pestle. Transfer the coriander and garlic mixture to a bowl. Add the fish sauce, lemon juice and sugar and stir well.

3. Cut the squid lengthways into quarters.

4. Finely cut the squid quarters crossways, then cut into strips about 5 cm/2 inches long and 1 cm/½ inch wide.

5. Blanch the squid in boiling water for 1 minute. Strain immediately and drain on kitchen paper.

6. Add the warm squid, the onions and chopped coriander to the bowl and toss in the sauce. Serve the salad lukewarm on a bed of lettuce leaves.

Three friends' salad

YAM SAM SAHAY

Luxurious • For guests

Serves 4
50 g/2 oz carrots
50 g/2 oz white cabbage
6–8 lettuce leaves
200 g/7 oz pork escalopes
200 g/7 oz boneless chicken
  breast, skinned
200 g/7 oz raw prawns
45 ml/3 tablespoons vegetable oil
30–45 ml/3 tablespoons water
45 ml/3 tablespoons roasted
  curry paste
45 ml/3 tablespoons fish sauce
45 ml/3 tablespoons sugar
45 ml/3 tablespoons lemon juice
50 g/2 oz cashew nuts, ground

Approximately per portion:
1,500 kj/360 kcal
34 g protein
18 g fat
16 g carbohydrate

● Approximate preparation
time: 1 hour

---

1. Cut the carrots into matchstick strips. Shred the white cabbage. Arrange the lettuce leaves around the edge of a large dish. Arrange carrots and the cabbage on top.

2. Cut the pork and the chicken into strips about 3 cm/1¼ inches long and 1 cm/½ inch wide. Peel and devein the prawns.

3. Heat 15 ml/1 tablespoon of the oil in a small frying pan. Add the pork and stir-fry over a medium heat for about 2 minutes. Remove from the heat and set aside to cool. Heat 15 ml/1 tablespoon of the remaining oil in another frying pan. Add the chicken and stir-fry over a medium heat for about 2 minutes. Remove from the heat and set aside to cool. Heat the remaining oil in another pan. Add the prawns and stir-fry for 1–2 minutes. Remove from the heat and set aside to cool. Arrange the 'three friends' alongside each other on the prepared dish.

4. Put the water in a small saucepan and bring to the boil. Stir in the curry paste, fish sauce and sugar and bring back to the boil. Remove from the heat and add the lemon juice and the cashew nuts. Set aside to cool. Pour the sauce over the meat and prawns and serve.

Above: Squid salad
Below: Three friends' salad

Beef salad

YAM NUA

Rather expensive

Serves 4
3 garlic cloves
5 fresh chillies
45 ml/3 tablespoons fish sauce
45 ml/3 tablespoons lemon juice
15 ml/1 tablespoon sugar
2 medium onions
1 bunch chives
1 sprig fresh coriander
500 g/1¼ lb sirloin of beef
30 ml/2 tablespoons vegetable oil

Approximately per portion:
1,200 kj/290 kcal
27 g protein
18 g fat
6 g carbohydrate

● Approximate preparation
  time: 50 minutes

---

1. Pound together the garlic and chillies in a mortar with a pestle. Transfer the mixture to a salad bowl. Stir in the fish sauce, lemon juice and sugar.

2. Thinly slice the onions, push out into rings, then cut the rings in half. Snip the chives into 3 cm/1¼ inch long pieces. Coarsely chop the fresh coriander.

3. Trim the beef and cut into 2 cm/¾ inch thick steaks. Heat the oil in a large frying pan and fry the steaks over a high heat for about 3 minutes on each side. Remove the beef from the heat and set aside to cool, then cut the steaks into thin strips.

4. Add the strips of beef, onions, chives and coriander to the salad bowl and toss well in the dressing. Serve immediately.

Cellophane noodle salad with meat and prawns

YAM WUNSEN

Easy to make

Serves 4
1 medium onion
1 bunch chives
1 sprig fresh coriander
5 dried wood ears
5 fresh chillies
45 ml/3 tablespoons fish sauce
45 ml/3 tablespoons lemon juice
15 ml/1 tablespoon sugar
115 g/4 oz cellophane noodles
115 g/4 oz raw or cooked prawns
115 g/4 oz minced pork

Approximately per portion:
640 kj/150 kcal
11 g protein
6 g fat
15 g carbohydrate

● Approximate preparation
  time: 50 minutes

---

1. Thinly slice the onion and push out into rings, then cut them in half. Snip the chives and coarsely chop the coriander.

2. Put the wood ears into a bowl and add sufficient hot water to cover. Set aside for about 20 minutes to soak. Drain and chop into small pieces.

3. Thinly slice the chillies. Put the chillies into a salad bowl, together with the fish sauce, lemon juice and sugar and stir until the sugar has dissolved.

4. Put the noodles in a bowl, cover with hot water and set aside for about 10 minutes to soften. Drain the noodles, then blanch in boiling water for about ½ minute. Refresh in cold water and drain well. Cut up the noodles with scissors. Peel and devein the prawns.

5. Add just enough water to cover the base of a medium-sized saucepan and bring to the boil. Add the pork and the prawns and cook, stirring constantly, for about 2–3 minutes, or until cooked through. Drain well.

6. Add the pork and prawn mixture and the noodles to the salad bowl, mix well and serve.

Tip

Wood ears are used less for their flavour than for their interesting texture. In fact, they do not have much flavour. They are often included in stir-fried meat and fish dishes to provide a contrast in colour.

Above: Beef salad
Below: Cellophane noodle salad with meat and prawns

Rice with tuna fish

KAO PAD PLA TUNA

Fried rice is very popular in Thailand and is prepared on every street corner in a variety of imaginative ways. To prevent the rice becoming sticky during frying, ensure that it has cooled completely first. It is often easiest to boil the rice the day before.

Serves 4
3 garlic cloves
1 sprig fresh coriander
150 g/5 oz can tuna fish
45 ml/3 tablespoons vegetable oil
150 g/5 oz mixed, frozen sweetcorn, peas and red peppers
750 g/1 lb 10 oz boiled rice, cooled (equivalent to 250 g/9 oz uncooked rice)
30 ml/2 tablespoons fish sauce
15 ml/1 tablespoon light soy sauce
salt
freshly ground black pepper
Simple chilli sauce, to serve

Approximately per portion:
1,800 kj/430 kcal
16 g protein
17 g fat
52 g carbohydrate

●Approximate preparation time: 30 minutes

1. Finely chop the garlic. Coarsely chop the coriander.

2. Drain and flake the tuna.

3. Heat the oil in a large frying pan and stir-fry the garlic for

1–2 minutes, until golden brown. Add the tuna and the mixed vegetables and stir-fry over a medium heat for about 2 minutes. Add the rice, fish sauce and soy sauce and stir-fry for a further 2 minutes. Season the rice with salt and pepper to taste, transfer to serving plates and sprinkle over the coriander. Serve with Simple chilli sauce (recipe on page 10).

Rice with pineapple

KAO PAD SAPPAROT

Easy to make

Serves 4
2 medium onions
2 tomatoes
580 g/1¼ lb can pineapple pieces
3 garlic cloves
45 ml/3 tablespoons vegetable oil
2 eggs
45 ml/3 tablespoons raisins
750g/1 lb 10 oz boiled rice, cooled (equivalent to 250 g/9 oz uncooked rice)
30 ml/2 tablespoons fish sauce
30 ml/2 tablespoons tomato ketchup
5 ml/1 teaspoon sugar
Chilli sauce with coriander, to serve

Approximately per portion:
2,200 kj/520 kcal
10 g protein
12 g fat
93 g carbohydrate

● Approximate preparation time: 30 minutes

1. Dice the onions and tomatoes.

2. Drain the pineapple. Finely chop the garlic.

3. Heat the oil in a large frying pan, add the garlic and stir-fry for 1–2 minutes, until golden brown. Add the eggs, stir in the pan and fry over a medium heat until they are just set.

4. Add the onions and fry for about 1 minute. Add the tomatoes, pineapple pieces, raisins and rice and stir-fry until heated through. Stir in the fish sauce, ketchup and sugar. Transfer to serving plates and serve immediately with Chilli sauce with coriander (recipe on page 10).

Tip

You can use fresh rather than canned pineapple. Cut the pineapple in half lengthways, scoop out the flesh with a spoon, then dice. Reserve the shells. Heat the 2 pineapple shells in an oven at 200°C/400°F/Gas 6 and serve the rice in them.

Above: Rice with pineapple
Below: Rice with tuna fish

Rice with prawns

KAO PAD GUNG

Famous recipe

Serves 4
500 g/1¼ lb raw tiger prawns
30 ml/2 tablespoons light soy sauce
2.5 ml/½ teaspoon freshly ground
  black pepper
2 medium onions
2 spring onions
3 garlic cloves
1 cucumber
45 ml/3 tablespoons vegetable oil
750 g/1 lb 10 oz boiled rice,
  cooled (equivalent to 250 g/9 oz
  uncooked rice)
30 ml/2 tablespoons fish sauce
30 ml/2 tablespoons tomato
  ketchup
5 ml/1 teaspoon sugar
Chilli sauce with coriander, to serve

Approximately per portion:
1,900 kj/450 kcal
30 g protein
11 g fat
56 g carbohydrate

● Approximate preparation
  time: 40 minutes

Variation

Instead of prawns, you can use
300 g/11 oz lean pork or 300 g/
11 oz boneless, skinned chicken
breasts cut into thin strips.

1. Remove the heads from the prawns, then peel them, leaving the tails intact, and devein. Mix the prawns with the soy sauce and pepper and set aside to marinate for 10 minutes.

2. Thinly slice the onions and push out into rings. Cut the spring onions in half lengthways and then into pieces 3 cm/1¼ inches long. Finely chop the garlic. Peel the cucumber and cut into 5 mm/ ¼ inch thick slices.

3. Heat the oil in a large frying pan. Stir-fry the garlic for 1 minute, until golden brown. Add the prawns and stir-fry over a high heat for about 1 minute, until they are red. Add the onion rings and stir-fry for about 1 minute.

4. Add the rice, spring onions, fish sauce, tomato ketchup and sugar and stir-fry until heated through. Transfer to serving plates, garnish with the cucumber slices and serve with Chilli sauce with coriander (recipe on page 10).

Rice noodles with broccoli

PAD SII LU

Cheap • Easy to make

Serves 4
200 g/7 oz rice noodles
200 g/7 oz lean pork
200 g/7 oz broccoli
4 garlic cloves
45 ml/3 tablespoons vegetable oil
2 eggs
30 ml/2 tablespoons fish sauce
30 ml/2 tablespoons light soy sauce
1 tablespoon sugar
freshly ground black pepper

Approximately per portion:
1,700 kj/400 kcal
23 g protein
16 g fat
42 g carbohydrate

● Approximate preparation
  time: 30 minutes

1. Cook the noodles in boiling water for about 3 minutes. Drain, refresh with cold water and drain again thoroughly.

2. Cut the pork into thin strips across the grain. Cut the broccoli into florets. Peel the stalks, remove and discard any tough pieces and dice the stalks finely. Finely chop the garlic.

3. Heat the oil in a frying pan over a medium heat. Add the garlic and stir-fry for 1–2 minutes, until golden brown. Add the pork strips and stir-fry for about 1 minute. Push the meat to one side of the pan. Break the eggs into the pan and stir-fry until they are golden. Mix together with the meat.

4. Add the broccoli and stir-fry for about 3 minutes. Add the noodles, fish sauce, soy sauce and sugar and stir-fry until completely heated through. Transfer to serving plates and sprinkle with freshly ground black pepper.

Tip

During the meal, guests season their noodle dishes with vinegar, sugar and chilli powder, according to their own taste.

29

Egg noodles with beansprouts

BAMIE PAD

Quick • Easy to make

Serves 4
300 g/11 oz egg noodles
2 spring onions
3 garlic cloves
50 g/2 oz ham
45 ml/3 tablespoons vegetable oil
200 g/7 oz beansprouts
30 ml/2 tablespoons fish sauce
30 ml/2 tablespoons oyster sauce
15 ml/1 tablespoon sugar

Approximately per portion:
1,700 kj/400 kcal
16 g protein
15 g fat
61 g carbohydrate

● Approximate preparation
time: 20 minutes

---

1. Simmer the noodles in a large pan of boiling water for about 4 minutes or according to the instructions on the packet. Drain, refresh with cold water and drain again thoroughly.

2. Cut the spring onions in half lengthways and then into pieces about 3 cm/1¼ inches long. Finely chop the garlic. Dice the ham.

3. Heat the oil in a frying pan. Add the garlic and ham and stir-fry over a medium heat for about 1 minute. Add the noodles, mix together well and stir-fry for a further 1 minute.

4. Add the beansprouts, spring onions, fish sauce, oyster sauce, and sugar. Mix together carefully and cook until heated through. The beansprouts should still be crunchy. Serve immediately.

Rice noodles with minced meat

PAD NA MU SAB

Inexpensive

Serves 4
300g/11 oz rice noodles
2 medium onions
2 tomatoes
2 garlic cloves
1 bunch chives
90 ml/6 tablespoons vegetable oil
30 ml/2 tablespoons dark
  soy sauce
400 g/14 oz minced beef or pork
45 ml/3 tablespoons fish sauce
30 ml/2 tablespoons Chinese rice
  wine or dry sherry
30 ml/2 tablespoons sugar
250 ml/8 fl oz water
15 ml/1 tablespoon cornflour
freshly ground black pepper

Approximately per portion:
3,000 kj/710 kcal
32 g protein
37 g fat
66 g carbohydrate

● Approximate preparation
time: 40 minutes

---

1. Cook the noodles in boiling water for about 3 minutes. Drain, refresh under cold water and drain again thoroughly.

2. Roughly chop the onions. Dice the tomatoes. Finely chop the garlic. Snip the chives.

3. Heat 45 ml/3 tablespoons of the oil in a large frying pan and add the rice noodles and soy sauce, Stir-fry over a high heat for about 1 minute. Divide between 4 serving plates and keep warm.

4. Add the remaining oil to the pan. Stir-fry the garlic for 1–2 minutes, until golden brown. Add the meat and the onions and stir-fry over a medium heat for about 2 minutes. Add the tomatoes, fish sauce, Chinese rice wine or dry sherry, sugar and all but 30 ml/ 2 tablespoons of the water. Cook for a further 1 minute.

5. Stir the cornflour with the remaining water to make a smooth paste and stir it into the sauce until it thickens. Pour the sauce over the noodles, season well with black pepper, garnish with the chives and serve immediately.

Tip

Season with chilli powder to your taste at the table.
  Chinese rice wine is available from many supermarkets and from Chinese food stores. Shaoxing is said to be the best. Dry sherry is a good substitute. Do not confuse rice wine with rice wine vinegar.

Above: Egg noodles with beansprouts
Below: Rice noodles with minced meat

Chicken with bamboo shoots

GANG KIAU WAN

Easy to make

Serves 4
400 g/14 oz boneless chicken
  breasts, skinned
2x 275 g/10 oz cans bamboo
  shoots
½ red pepper
400 ml/14 fl oz coconut milk
30 ml/2 tablespoons green
  curry paste
60 ml/4 tablespoons fish sauce
45 ml/3 tablespoons sugar
20 leaves Thai basil, to garnish

Approximately per portion:
810 kj/190 kcal
28 g protein
2 g fat
18 g carbohydrate

● Approximate preparation
  time: 30 minutes

---

1. Cut the chicken into thin strips. Cut the bamboo shoots into matchsticks. Core and seed the pepper and cut the flesh into matchstick strips.

2. Put 75 ml/5 tablespoons of the thick part of the coconut milk in a medium saucepan and bring to the boil. Reduce the heat, stir in the curry paste and simmer for about 1 minute. Add the chicken, bamboo shoots, fish sauce, sugar and the remaining coconut milk and simmer over a low heat, stirring occasionally, for about 10 minutes. If the sauce appears too thick, add a little water.

3. Transfer to a warmed serving dish, garnish with the strips of red pepper and the Thai basil leaves and serve immediately.

Variation
Instead of chicken you can use 400 g/14 oz lean, boneless pork.

Mussaman curry

GANG MUSSAMAN

Famous recipe

Serves 4
500 g/1¼ lb braising steak
4 medium potatoes
2 medium onions
400 ml/14 fl oz coconut milk
45 ml/3 tablespoons Mussaman
  curry paste
60 ml/4 tablespoons palm sugar or
  soft brown sugar
60 ml/4 tablespoons fish sauce
30 ml/2 tablespoons lemon juice
45 ml/3 tablespoons roasted
  peanuts
1 bay leaf
500 ml/17 fl oz water

Approximately per portion:
1,400 kj/330 kcal
29 g protein
12 g fat
29 g carbohydrate

● Approximate preparation
  time: 2 hours

---

1. Trim the steak and cut into 2 cm/¾ inch cubes. Cut the potatoes into quarters. Cut the onions in half.

2. Put 75 ml/5 tablespoons of the thick part of the coconut milk into a large pan and bring to the boil. Stir in the curry paste and cook for about 1 minute. Add the beef, the remaining coconut milk, the sugar, fish sauce, lemon juice, peanuts, bay leaf and water.

3. Lower the heat, partially cover the pan and simmer over a low heat for about 50 minutes. Add the potatoes and the onions, partially cover and simmer for a further 40 minutes.

4. Remove and discard the bay leaf and serve the curry immediately.

Variation
You can also prepare this dish with 750 g/1 lb 10 oz chicken portions. Reduce the cooking time to a total of 40 minutes.

Tip

To make Mussaman curry paste, seed 12 dried chillies and soak in hot water for 15 minutes. Mix together 5 garlic cloves, 60 ml/4 tablespoons chopped shallots, 1 lemon grass stalk, 10 ml/2 teaspoons chopped galangal, 5 ml/1 teaspoon cumin seeds, 15 ml/1 tablespoon coriander seeds, 2 cloves and 4 black peppercorns. Dry-fry over a low heat for 5 minutes. Grind together the spice mixture and the chillies in a mortar with a pestle or in a food processor. Stir in 5 ml/1 teaspoon sugar, 30 ml/2 tablespoons vegetable oil and salt to taste.

Above: Chicken with bamboo shoots
Below: Mussaman curry

Pork with basil

PANANG MU

Famous recipe • Quick

Serves 4
500 g/1¼ lb boneless, lean pork
½ red pepper
3 kaffir lime leaves
200 ml/7 fl oz coconut milk
45 ml/3 tablespoons Panang
* curry paste*
30 ml/2 tablespoons fish sauce
30 ml/2 tablespoons sugar
20 leaves Thai basil

Approximately per portion:
1,000 kj/240 kcal
27 g protein
11 g fat
9 g carbohydrate

● Approximate preparation
time: 25 minutes

---

1. Cut the pork into thin slices across the grain. Core and seed the pepper and cut the flesh into matchsticks. Cut the kaffir lime leaves into very fine strips.

2. Set aside 15 ml/1 tablespoon of the thick part of the coconut milk. Put the remainder into a medium saucepan and bring to the boil. Reduce the heat, stir in the curry paste and simmer gently for about 1 minute.

3. Add the pork, fish sauce, sugar and kaffir lime leaves and simmer gently for about 5 minutes. Transfer to a warmed serving dish, garnish with the basil leaves, strips of red pepper and reserved coconut milk.

Variation

As an alternative, you can also use 500 g/1¼ lb of peeled and deveined raw prawns.

Pork with pineapple

GANG KUA SAPPAROT

Easy to make

Serves 4
400 g/14 oz boneless, lean pork
4 kaffir lime leaves
2 x 270 g/9½ oz cans pineapple
* pieces*
400 ml/14 fl oz coconut milk
45 ml/3 tablespoons red curry paste
45 ml/3 tablespoons palm sugar or
* soft brown sugar*
45 ml/3 tablespoons fish sauce
45 ml/3 tablespoons lemon juice
salt
freshly ground black pepper

Approximately per portion:
1,400 kj/330 kcal
23 g protein
9 g fat
41 g carbohydrate

● Approximate preparation
time: 30 minutes

---

1. Cut the pork into thin strips across the grain. Cut the kaffir lime leaves into quarters. Drain the pineapple pieces and reserve 120 ml/4 fl oz of the juice.

2. Put 75 ml/5 tablespoons of the thick part of the coconut milk in a medium-sized saucepan and bring to the boil. Boil for 1 minute,

reduce the heat, then stir in the red curry paste and simmer for a further 1 minute.

3. Add the pork and cook for a further 2 minutes. Add the pineapple, sugar, fish sauce, kaffir lime leaves, lemon juice and the remaining coconut milk. Stir in the reserved pineapple juice and simmer over a low heat for about 5 minutes. Season to taste with salt and freshly ground black pepper and add more sugar or lemon juice if desired. Serve immediately.

Tip

To make red curry paste, dry-fry 5 ml/1 teaspoon cumin seeds and 30 ml/2 tablespoons coriander seeds over a low heat for 2 minutes. Pound the seeds with 2.5 ml/½ teaspoon ground nutmeg, 2.5 ml/½ teaspoon ground cinnamon. 1.5 ml/¼ teaspoon ground cloves and 15 ml/1 tablespoon paprika. Pound together 5 fresh red chillies, 30 ml/2 tablespoons sugar and a pinch of salt. Mix together the ground spices, chilli paste, 1 shredded lemon grass stalk, 3 crushed garlic cloves, a finely chopped 2.5 cm/1 inch piece galangal, 3 finely chopped shallots, 50g/2 oz finely chopped coriander roots or stems and 30 ml/2 tablespoons vegetable oil. Store in a screw-top jar in the refrigerator.

Above: Pork with basil
Below: Pork with pineapple

Pork with garlic

MU TOD GRATHIAM PRIKTHAI

Easy to make

Serves 4–6
1 kg/2½ lb boneless, lean pork
10 garlic cloves
5 ml/1 teaspoon black pepper
30 ml/2 tablespoons fish sauce
15 ml/1 tablespoon dark soy sauce
1 cucumber
5 tablespoons vegetable oil
Simple chilli sauce, to serve

For 6, per portion about:
1,500 kj/360 kcal
36 g protein
22 g fat
4 g carbohydrate

● Approximate preparation
time: 1½ hours (1 hour
marinating time)

---

1. Cut the pork across the grain into strips about 4 cm/1½ inches long and 2 cm/¾ inch wide.

2. Pound together the garlic and pepper in a mortar with a pestle, then mix together with the fish sauce and soy sauce in a shallow dish. Add the pork and toss well to coat. Cover and set aside in the refrigerator to marinate for 1 hour.

3. Peel and thinly slice the cucumber.

4. Heat the oil in a frying pan until very hot. Remove the pork from the marinade, add to the pan and stir-fry until it is well browned and cooked through.

5. Arrange the cucumber slices around the edge of a serving dish and pile the meat in the middle. Serve immediately with Simple chilli sauce (recipe on page 10).

Tip

Drink a glass of cold milk after eating this dish; then you will not smell so strongly of garlic the next day!

Chicken with ginger

GAI PAD KHING

Famous recipe

Serves 4
5 dried wood ears
75 ml/5 tablespoons vegetable oil
115 g/4 oz unsalted cashew nuts
2 x 6 cm/2½ inch pieces fresh root ginger
3 spring onions
2 tomatoes
400 g/14 oz boneless chicken breasts, skinned
3 garlic cloves
30 ml/2 tablespoons vegetable oil
30 ml/2 tablespoons fish sauce
30 ml/2 tablespoons oyster sauce
15 ml/1 tablespoon sugar
salt • freshly ground black pepper

Approximately per portion:
1,800 kj/430 kcal
29 g protein
29 g fat
14 g carbohydrate

● Approximate preparation
time: 40 minutes

---

1. Put the wood ears in a bowl, cover with hot water and set aside to soak for about 20 minutes.

2. Heat the oil in a frying pan. Add the cashew nuts and stir-fry for 2–3 minutes, until golden brown. Remove the nuts from the pan and drain on kitchen paper.

3. Cut the ginger into thin strips. Squeeze out the wood ears, remove and discard the stalks and cut the wood ears into quarters. Cut the spring onions into pieces about 3 cm/1¼ inches long. Cut the tomatoes into quarters.

4. Cut the chicken breast into strips about 3 cm/1¼ inches long and 1 cm/½ inch wide. Finely chop the garlic.

5. Heat the oil in a frying pan and stir-fry the garlic for 1–2 minutes, until golden brown. Add the chicken and stir-fry for about 2 minutes over a high heat.

6. Add the ginger, wood ears, tomatoes, spring onions and the cashew nuts and stir-fry over a high heat for about 2 minutes. Reduce the heat, add the fish sauce, oyster sauce and sugar. Mix well, season to taste with salt and pepper and heat through. Serve immediately.

Above: Pork with garlic
Below: Chicken with ginger

Chicken breast with chillies

PAD KIMAU GAI

Quick • Easy to make

Serves 4
700 g/1½ lb boneless chicken
   breasts, skinned
15 ml/1 tablespoon fish sauce
5 fresh red Thai chillies
3 garlic cloves
45 ml/3 tablespoons vegetable oil
30 ml/2 tablespoons light soy sauce
30 ml/2 tablespoons oyster sauce
15 ml/1 tablespoon sugar
20 Thai basil leaves, to garnish

Approximately per portion:
1,100 kj/260 kcal
41 g protein
9 g fat
5 g carbohydrate

● Approximate preparation
   time: 30 minutes

Variation
Instead of chicken breast you can use minced pork.

1. Cut the chicken breast into very thin slices, then chop finely. Mix together with the fish sauce and set aside to marinate for about 10 minutes.

2. Meanwhile pound together the chillies and garlic in a mortar with a pestle to make a smooth paste.

3. Heat the oil in a frying pan. Add the garlic and chilli paste and the chopped chicken and stir-fry over a medium heat for about 1 minute. Stir in the soy sauce, oyster sauce and sugar. Cook, stirring, for about 2 minutes. If the mixture becomes too sticky or looks as if it might burn, add a little water.

4. Finally, add the basil leaves and season, if liked, with a little more soy or oyster sauce.

Liver with Chinese chives

PAD DOK GUISHAI

Quick

Serves 4
400 g/14 oz Chinese chives
400 g/14 oz lamb's or pig's liver
3 garlic cloves
45 ml/3 tablespoons vegetable oil
30 ml/2 tablespoons fish sauce
30 ml/2 tablespoons oyster sauce
15 ml/1 tablespoon sugar

Approximately per portion:
1,100 kj/260 kcal
25 g protein
14 g fat
10 g carbohydrate

● Approximate preparation
  time: 20 minutes

Variation
As an alternative you can also use
400 g/14 oz peeled and deveined
raw prawns instead of the liver.
The cooking time remains
unchanged.

1. Trim off the bulbous roots of
the Chinese chives and cut the
green leaves into 4 cm/1½ inch
long pieces.

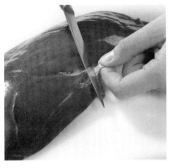

2. Trim the liver and cut into strips
about 3 cm/1¼ inches long and
5 mm/¼ inch wide.

3. Finely chop the garlic. Heat the
oil in a large frying pan and stir-fry
the garlic for 1–2 minutes, until
golden brown. Add the liver and
stir-fry over a high heat for about
3 minutes.

4. Add the Chinese chives, fish
sauce, oyster sauce and sugar and
cook the liver for about 1 further
minute. Season with more fish
sauce or oyster sauce, if desired,
and serve immediately.

Baked chicken

GAI YANG

Easy to make

Serves 4
6 garlic cloves
5 ml/1 teaspoon freshly ground
    black pepper
8 chicken legs
45 ml/3 tablespoons dark soy sauce
15 ml/1 tablespoon fish sauce
vegetable oil, for greasing
Simple chilli sauce, to serve

Approximately per portion:
1,300 kj/310 kcal
47 g protein
12 g fat
2 g carbohydrate

● Approximate preparation
   time: 1½ hours (1 hour
   marinating time)

---

1. Coarsely chop the garlic, then
pound, together with the pepper,
in a mortar with a pestle.

2. Coat the chicken legs with the
garlic paste and place in a shallow
dish. Add the soy sauce and fish
sauce and turn to coat. Cover and
set aside in the refrigerator to
marinate for about 1 hour.

3. Preheat oven to 190°C/375°F/
Gas 5. Line a baking sheet with
aluminium foil and brush with oil.
Arrange the chicken legs on the
prepared baking sheet in a single
layer. Bake in the oven for about
30 minutes, turning the legs and
brushing with the marinade
occasionally. Serve with Simple
chilli sauce (recipe on page 10).

Tip

This recipe is equally delicious
with chicken wings or breasts.
It is also excellent cooked on a
barbecue. In this case, wipe off
and reserve the marinade
before you put the chicken legs
on the barbecue grill to avoid
splashing the charcoal and
causing it to flare up
dangerously. Brush with the
marinade when the chicken legs
have begun to cook, taking care
not to splash it on the charcoal.

Pork with cucumber

PAD TANGKWAH SEI KHAI

Easy to prepare • Quick

Serves 4
2 medium cucumbers
2 spring onions
400 g/14 oz boneless, lean pork,
    such as tenderloin
3 garlic cloves
45 ml/3 tablespoons vegetable oil
45 ml/3 tablespoons fish sauce
45 ml/3 tablespoons oyster sauce
15 ml/1 tablespoon sugar
2 eggs

Approximately per portion:
1,300 kj/310 kcal
27 g protein • 19 g fat
9 g carbohydrate

● Approximate preparation
   time: 20 minutes

---

1. Peel the cucumbers and cut into
5 mm/¼ inch dice. Cut the spring
onions in half lengthways and then
cut the halves into pieces about
3 cm/1¼ inch long.

2. Cut the pork across the grain
into strips about 3 cm/1¼ inches
long and 5 mm/¼ inch wide. Finely
chop the garlic.

3. Heat the oil in a frying pan or
wok and stir-fry the garlic for
1–2 minutes, until golden brown.
Add the pork and stir-fry over a
high heat for about 2 minutes. Stir
in the cucumbers, spring onions,
fish sauce, oyster sauce and sugar.
Stir-fry for about 1 more minute. If
the mixture becomes too thick,
add a little water.

4. Break the eggs and add to the
pan. Cook, stirring constantly, until
the eggs have set. Season with
more fish sauce or oyster sauce, if
liked, and serve.

Above: Baked chicken
Below: Pork with cucumber

Sweet-and-sour chicken

GAI PAD PRIAU WAN

Sweet- and-sour is a classic combination throughout South-east Asian cookery. It epitomizes the quality of balance and contrast that is characteristic of Thai and Chinese cuisines.

Serves 4
300 g/11 oz boneless chicken
*   breasts, skinned*
30 ml/2 tablespoons light soy
*   sauce*
freshly ground black pepper
2 medium tomatoes
2 medium onions
½ cucumber
1 red pepper
300 g/11 oz can pineapple
*   pieces*
3 garlic cloves
90/3½ oz g tempura flour or
*   plain flour*
250 ml/8 fl oz water
15 ml/1 tablespoon cornflour
45 ml/3 tablespoons sunflower oil
75 ml/5 tablespoons tomato
*   ketchup*
45 ml/3 tablespoons fish sauce
45 ml/3 tablespoons Chinese rice
*   wine or dry sherry*
60 ml/4 tablespoons sugar
oil, for deep-frying

Approximately per portion:
2,600 kj/620 kcal
21 g protein
34 g fat
60 g carbohydrate

● Approximate preparation
   time: 1 hour

---

1. Cut the chicken into 2 cm/ ¾ inch cubes and place in a shallow dish. Mix together the soy sauce and pepper and pour over the chicken cubes, turning to coat thoroughly. Set aside in the refrigerator to marinate for about 30 minutes.

2. Meanwhile cut the tomatoes into quarters. Dice the onions. Peel and dice the cucumber. Core, seed and dice the pepper. Drain the pineapple pieces and reserve 120 ml/4 fl oz of the juice. Finely chop the garlic.

3. Heat the oil for deep-frying in a deep-fryer or wok. Mix together the flour and water to make a fairly thick, smooth batter. Add more water, if necessary. Remove the chicken cubes from the marinade and coat in the batter. Fry the chicken cubes in batches, until golden brown. Remove and drain on kitchen paper. Keep the fried chicken warm while you cook the remaining batches.

4. Mix together the cornflour and 15–30 ml/1–2 tablespoons of the reserved pineapple juice in a small bowl to make a smooth paste. Heat the sunflower oil in a large frying pan. Add the garlic and stir-fry over a medium heat for 1–2 minutes, until golden brown. Add the onions, cucumber, red pepper and pineapple and stir-fry over a very high heat for about 3 minutes.

5. Stir in the tomato ketchup and the fish sauce and reduce the heat. Add the tomatoes and the remaining pineapple juice and bring to the boil.

6. Stir in the Chinese rice wine or dry sherry and the sugar. Stir the cornflour paste again, then stir it into the pan. Bring to the boil once again, stirring constantly, and cook until the sauce thickens.

7. Transfer the mixture to a serving bowl and arrange the chicken on top. Serve immediately.

Variation
Instead of chicken breast you can use turkey breast.

Tip

Once this dish is ready, do not allow it to stand for very long. Otherwise the crisp outside of the chicken becomes soggy and does not taste so delicious.

Tender chicken fried in crisp batter and served in a rich sauce is an ideal meal for guests because everyone likes sweet-and-sour chicken.

Beef with oyster sauce

NUA PAD NAM MANHOY

For guests

Serves 4
500 g/1¼ lb rump steak
30 ml/2 tablespoons dark soy sauce
pinch of freshly ground black pepper
15 ml/1 tablespoon flour
5 dried Shiitake mushrooms
300 g/11 oz oyster mushrooms
2 spring onions
1 red pepper
5 cm/2 inch piece fresh root ginger
4 garlic cloves
45 ml/3 tablespoons vegetable oil
75 ml/5 tablespoons oyster sauce
15 ml/1 tablespoon fish sauce
5 ml/1 teaspoon sugar
60 ml/4 tablespoons Chinese rice
  wine or dry sherry

Approximately per portion:
1,500 kj/360 kcal
29 g protein
21 g fat
7 g carbohydrate

● Approximate preparation
  time: 1½ hours (1 hour
  marinating time)

---

1. Cut the steak into bite-size pieces and place in a dish. Mix together the soy sauce, black pepper and flour and pour over the steak .Set aside in the refrigerator to marinate for 1 hour.

2. Put the Shiitake mushrooms in a bowl, cover with warm water and set aside for about 20 minutes. Then squeeze out the water and cut the mushrooms into quarters.

3. Tear the oyster mushrooms into bite-size pieces. Cut the spring onions in half lengthways and then into pieces about 3 cm/1¼ inches long. Core the pepper and cut into matchstick strips. Finely chop the ginger and garlic.

4. Heat the oil in a frying pan until very hot. Stir-fry the garlic, ginger and meat over a high heat for about 5 minutes. Lower the heat, add the shiitake and oyster mushrooms, spring onions, oyster sauce, fish sauce and sugar and stir-fry for a further 3 minutes.

5. Stir in the rice wine or sherry. Transfer to a serving dish, garnish with the red pepper and serve.

Cold white noodles

KANOM DIEN SAO NAM

Sophisticated

This cold noodle dish is very popular when it gets very hot in Thailand just before the rainy season.

Serves 4
350 g/12 oz somen noodles
4 x 5 cm/2 inch pieces fresh
  root ginger
10 garlic cloves
2 x 270 g/9½ oz cans pineapple
  pieces
90 ml/6 tablespoons dried shrimps
4 fresh chillies
60 ml/4 tablespoons lemon juice
60 ml/4 tablespoons fish sauce
60 ml/4 tablespoons sugar
400 ml/14 fl oz coconut milk
5 ml/1 teaspoon cornflour

Approximately per portion:
2,300 kj/550 kcal
21 g protein
4 g fat
110 g carbohydrate

● Approximate preparation
  time: 30 minutes

---

1. Cook the noodles in boiling water for about 4 minutes, then refresh in cold water. Take a small portion of the noodles and shape into a nest in your hand and gently press out. Make nests with the remaining noodles in the same way. Set aside.

2. Cut the ginger into thin strips about 2 cm/¾ inch long. Finely chop the garlic. Drain and finely chop the pineapple pieces. Put them in 3 separate small serving bowls.

3. Put the dried shrimps into a food processor and work until very finely chopped. Transfer to a small serving bowl. Cut the chillies into rings. Mix together the chillies, lemon juice, fish sauce and sugar in another small serving bowl.

4. Put the coconut milk in a small saucepan. Add the cornflour and bring to the boil, stirring constantly. Remove the pan from the heat and set aside to cool, then transfer to another small serving bowl.

5. Arrange the noodles on a serving plate and serve with the small bowls of accompaniments. At the table all the guests help themselves to cold noodles, garlic, ginger, shrimps, coconut cream and chilli sauce.

Above: Beef with oyster sauce
Below: Cold white noodles

Bamboo shoots with eggs

PAD NOHMAY SEI KAI

Quick

Serves 4
2 x 270 g/9½ oz cans bamboo
  shoots
3 spring onions
3 garlic cloves
45 ml/3 tablespoons vegetable oil
30 ml/2 tablespoons fish sauce
30 ml/2 tablespoons oyster sauce
15 ml/1 tablespoon sugar
2 eggs
Chilli sauce with coriander, to serve

Approximately per portion:
760 kj/180 kcal
8 g protein
11 g fat
13 g carbohydrate

● Approximate preparation
  time: 20 minutes

---

1. Cut the bamboo shoots into matchstick strips. Cut the spring onions in half lengthways and then into pieces about 3 cm/1¼ inches long. Finely chop the garlic.

2. Heat the oil in a frying pan or wok and stir-fry the garlic over a medium heat for 1–2 minutes, until golden brown. Add the bamboo shoots, spring onions, fish sauce, oyster sauce and sugar and stir-fry over a medium heat for about 3 minutes.

3. Push the vegetables to one side of the pan, break the eggs into the pan and cook, stirring until they are just set. Try to avoid letting them come into contact with the vegetables while they are cooking.

4. Mix the eggs with the vegetables and serve with Chilli sauce with coriander (recipe on page 10).

Stir-fried mixed vegetables

PAD PAK RUAMIT

Easy to make

Serves 4
200 g/7 oz broccoli
150 g/5 oz French beans
200 g/7 oz baby corn cobs
200 g/7 oz pak choi
300 g/11 oz baby carrots
3 spring onions
5 garlic cloves
75 ml/5 tablespoons vegetable oil
45 ml/3 tablespoons fish sauce
45 ml/3 tablespoons oyster sauce
15 ml/1 tablespoon sugar
60 ml/4 tablespoons Chinese rice
  wine or dry sherry

Approximately per portion:
1,100 kj/260 kcal
8 g protein
14 g fat
25 g carbohydrate

● Approximate preparation
  time: 40 minutes

---

1. Cut the broccoli into florets, peel the stalks and cut into matchstick strips. Trim the beans and cut into quarters. Cut the baby corn cobs in half crossways.

Cut the pak choi into bite-size pieces. Cut the carrots lengthways into quarters and then crossways into quarters. Cut the spring onions in half lengthways and then into pieces about 3 cm/1¼ inches long.

2. Finely chop the garlic. Heat the oil in a large frying pan or wok over a high heat. Stir-fry the garlic for 1–2 minutes, until golden brown. Add the broccoli, carrots, beans and corn cobs and stir-fry over a high heat for about 3 minutes. Stir in the spring onions, pak choi, fish sauce, oyster sauce and sugar.

3. Add the rice wine or dry sherry and cook, stirring and tossing the vegetables constantly, for a further 2 minutes, until the vegetables are cooked but still crunchy.

Variation
You can use any kinds of vegetables that happen to be in season in this recipe. Asparagus, spinach, mushrooms, celery and cauliflower are particularly suitable for this dish.

Above: Stir-fried mixed vegetables
Below: Bamboo shoots with eggs

Mussels with lemon grass

HOY MANG PU OB

Quick

Serves 4
2 kg/4½ lb mussels
2 lemon grass stalks
5 cm/ 2 inch piece galangal
5 kaffir lime leaves
3 shallots
500 ml/17 fl oz water
2.5 ml/½ teaspoon salt
Chilli sauce with coriander,
   to serve

Approximately per portion:
550 kj/130 kcal
18 g protein
2 g fat
8 g carbohydrate

● Approximate preparation
   time: 20 minutes

---

1. Scrub and debeard the mussels under cold running water. Discard any that do not close immediately when sharply tapped.

2. Cut the lemon grass stalks in half. Crush the lemon grass and the galangal with the blade of a heavy knife. Cut the kaffir lime leaves into quarters. Cut the shallots in half.

3. Put the lemon grass, kaffir lime leaves, galangal, shallots, water, salt and mussels into a large saucepan and bring to the boil over a high heat. Cover and cook over a high heat for about 5 minutes, until the shells open. Discard any mussels that remain closed.

4. Remove and discard the kaffir lime leaves, lemon grass stalks and galangal. Transfer the mussels to a serving dish and serve immediately with Chilli sauce with coriander (recipe on page 10).

Stuffed squid

PLA MUK YAD SAI

For guests • Sophisticated

Serves 4
5 cm/2 inch piece fresh root ginger
2 spring onions
7 dried shiitake mushrooms
1 sprig fresh coriander with root
5 garlic cloves
2.5 ml/½ teaspoon freshly ground
   black pepper
350 g/12 oz minced pork
30 ml/2 tablespoons dark soy sauce
1 egg
salt
20 medium-sized squid, cleaned
60 ml/4 tablespoons vegetable oil
45 ml/3 tablespoons oyster sauce
30 ml/2 tablespoons fish sauce
15 ml/1 tablespoon sugar

Approximately per portion:
1,900 kj/450 kcal
37 g protein
30 g fat
7 g carbohydrate

● Approximate preparation
   time: 40 minutes

---

1. Finely chop the ginger. Cut the spring onions in half lengthways, then cut into pieces about 3 cm/1¼ inches long.

2. Put the shiitake mushrooms in a bowl, cover with hot water and set aside to soak for about 20 minutes. Squeeze out the mushrooms and cut into quarters. Reserve the soaking water.

3. Cut off the coriander root, remove the leaves from the stems and set aside. Pound together the coriander root, 2 of the garlic cloves and the pepper in a mortar with a pestle. Put the pork in a bowl and mix in the coriander and garlic paste, soy sauce and the egg and season to taste with salt.

4. Carefully stuff the squid with the pork mixture. Finely chop the remaining garlic.

5. Heat the oil in a frying pan. Stir-fry the garlic and the ginger briefly. Add the stuffed squid and fry over a medium heat, turning frequently, until golden on all sides. Add the mushrooms, oyster sauce, fish sauce, sugar and the reserved soaking water.

6. Lower the heat, cover and cook for about 5 minutes. Add the spring onions, bring to the boil and cook for a further 1 minute. Transfer to a serving dish, garnish with the coriander leaves and serve immediately.

Above: Mussels with lemon grass
Below: Stuffed squid

Tiger prawns with garlic

KUNG KRATHIAM PRIG THAI

Rather expensive

Serves 4
12 raw tiger prawns
10 garlic cloves
5 ml/1 teaspoon salt
5 ml/1 teaspoon black pepper
*30 ml/2 tablespoons lemon
    juice*
3 medium tomatoes
1 cucumber
1 bunch chives
50 g/2 oz butter
120 ml/4 fl oz water

Approximately per portion:
1,100 kj/260 kcal
30 g protein
13 g fat
7 g carbohydrate

● Approximate preparation
   time: 30 minutes

1. Remove and discard the heads from the prawns. Peel the prawns, leaving the tails intact, and devein. Finely chop the garlic.

2. In a bowl mix together the prawns, garlic, salt, pepper and lemon juice. Set aside in the refrigerator to marinate.

3. Cut the tomatoes into slices about 5 mm/¼ inch thick. Peel and cut the cucumber into slices about 5 mm/¼ inch thick. Snip the chives. Arrange the tomato and cucumber slices around the edge of a large serving dish.

4. Melt the butter in a frying pan or wok over a low heat. Add the prawns to the pan. Add the water to the bowl which contained the prawns and marinade, stir, then add to the frying pan. Cover the pan and cook over a medium heat for about 3–4 minutes, until the prawns have turned pink.

5. Transfer the prawns to the serving dish with the tomato and cucumber slices, garnish with the chives and serve.

Tip

If using frozen raw prawns, thaw them thoroughly and then pat dry on kitchen paper before cooking, as they have a tendency to become soggy.

Mixed seafood

PAD TALEE

Exclusive

Obtain a mixture of fresh seafood, such as raw prawns, squid and snapper or mullet fillets, from your fishmonger or supermarket. It is quicker and easier if they are already prepared for cooking.

Serves 4
800g/1¾ lb mixed seafood, cleaned
3 garlic cloves
1 green pepper • 1 red pepper
60 ml/4 tablespoons vegetable oil
*30 ml/2 tablespoons roasted
    curry paste*
30 ml/2 tablespoons fish sauce
30 ml/2 tablespoons sugar
20 fresh Thai basil leaves

Approximately per portion:
1,200 kj/290 kcal
36 g protein
12 g fat
10 g carbohydrate

● Approximate preparation
   time: 30 minutes

1. Cut the fish fillets into bite-sized pieces. Thinly slice the squid crossways.

2. Finely chop the garlic. Core and seed the peppers and cut into matchstick strips.

3. Heat the oil in a frying pan over a medium heat. Stir-fry the garlic for 1–2 minutes, until golden brown. Stir in the curry paste. Add the strips of pepper.

4. Add the seafood, fish sauce and sugar, cover and cook over a medium heat for about 4 minutes. Stir in the basil leaves. Season with more fish sauce, if liked. Transfer to a warmed serving dish and serve immediately.

Above: Mixed seafood
Below: Tiger prawns with garlic

Baked fish

HOO MOG PLA

Unusual

Traditionally, fish is baked wrapped in banana leaves in Thailand. However, these are not always easy to obtain in the West, so a conventional ovenproof dish has been used here.

Serves 4
200 g/7 oz white cabbage
5 kaffir lime leaves
½ red pepper
500 g/1¼ lb fish fillets, such as
    monkfish, cod, snapper or pollack
4 garlic cloves
5 ml/1 teaspoon pepper
60 ml/4 tablespoons red curry paste
400 ml/14 fl oz coconut milk
1 egg
60 ml/4 tablespoons fish sauce
2.5 ml/½ teaspoon cornflour

Approximately per portion:
820 kj/200 kcal
27 g protein
7 g fat
7 g carbohydrate

● Approximate preparation
  time: 1 hour

1. Shred the white cabbage. Blanch in boiling water for about 1 minute, then drain thoroughly and pat dry with kitchen paper.

2. Cut the kaffir lime leaves into very fine strips. Core and seed the red pepper half and cut into matchstick strips.

3. Reserve 115 g/4 oz of the fish and cut the remainder diagonally into thick slices.

4. Put the garlic, the reserved fish and the pepper into a food processor and work to make a smooth purée. Transfer to a mixing bowl and stir in the curry paste. Reserve about 45 ml/3 tablespoons of the thick part of the coconut milk and beat the remainder into the fish purée with a hand-held electric mixer set at a low speed.

5. Preheat the oven to 180°C/350°F/Gas 4. Add the egg, kaffir lime leaves and fish sauce to the fish purée and beat for about 1 further minute. Stir in the slices of fish.

Tip

It is very easy to cut the fish fillet into neat and even-sized slices if you wrap it in kitchen foil and put it into the freezer for about 30 minutes beforehand. The white cabbage must be thoroughly dried, otherwise the dish will become watery. This baked fish dish also tastes delicious cold.

6. Arrange the cabbage on the base of an ovenproof dish and spoon over the fish mixture. Cover and bake in the oven for about 30 minutes.

7. Meanwhile mix the reserved coconut milk with the cornflour to make a smooth paste. Bring to the boil in a small pan, stirring once.

8. Remove the fish from the oven, garnish with the thick coconut milk and serve immediately.

Sea bream with Thai basil

PLA RAD PRIK

Quite expensive

Serves 4
2 x 500 g/1¼ lb sea bream, cleaned
   and scaled
5 ml/1 teaspoon salt
1 red pepper
1 green pepper
4 garlic cloves
3 fresh chillies
45 ml/3 tablespoons sunflower or
   safflower oil
45 ml/3 tablespoons fish sauce
45 ml/3 tablespoons white
   wine vinegar
45 ml/3 tablespoons palm sugar or
   soft brown sugar
30 Thai basil leaves
vegetable oil, for deep-frying

Approximately per portion:
2,700 kj/640 kcal
25 g protein
54 g fat
13 g carbohydrate

● Approximate preparation
   time: 45 minutes

---

1. Using a sharp knife, make 2 or 3 diagonal slashes in the skin on each side of the fish. Rub the insides and outsides of the sea bream with the salt.

2. Core and seed the red and green peppers and cut into matchstick strips. Set aside.

3. Pound together the garlic and chillies in a mortar with a pestle. Set aside.

4. Heat the vegetable oil in a large frying pan or wok. Fry the sea bream over a medium heat for about 20 minutes.

5. Five minutes before the end of the cooking time, heat the sunflower or safflower oil in a frying pan. Stir-fry the garlic and chilli paste for 1–2 minutes. Add the fish sauce, vinegar, sugar and peppers and stir-fry. If the sauce is too thick or looks as if it might burn, stir in a little water. Stir in the Thai basil.

6. Drain the sea bream on kitchen paper and arrange on a serving dish. Pour over the sauce and serve immediately.

Prawns with cellophane noodles

GUNG PAD WUNSEN

Famous recipe

Although this dish is prepared using noodles, rice is usually also served with it.

Serves 4
700 g/1½ lb raw prawns
30 ml/2 tablespoons light soy sauce
10 ml/2 teaspoons freshly ground
   black pepper
90 g/3½ oz cellophane noodles
90 g/3½ oz white cabbage
2 spring onions
1 beef tomato
2 garlic cloves
45 ml/3 tablespoons vegetable oil
30 ml/2 tablespoons fish sauce
30 ml/2 tablespoons oyster sauce
15 ml/1 tablespoon sugar

Approximately per portion:
1,300 kj/310 kcal
35 g protein
10 g fat
19 g carbohydrate

● Approximate preparation
   time: 40 minutes

---

1. Remove and discard the heads from the prawns. Peel the prawns, leaving the tails intact, and devein. Place them in a bowl with the soy sauce and the pepper and turn to coat. Set aside in the refrigerator to marinate.

2. Soak the noodles in hot water for 10 minutes to soften, then drain and cut up with scissors.

3. Cut the white cabbage into 2 cm/¾ inch squares. Cut the spring onions in half lengthways and then into pieces about 3 cm/1¼ inches long. Cut the tomato into 8 pieces.

4. Finely chop the garlic. Heat the oil in a frying pan and stir-fry the garlic for 1–2 minutes, until golden brown. Add the prawns and stir-fry over a high heat for about 1 minute, until their colour changes to pink. Add the cabbage and stir-fry for a further 1 minute.

5. Add the tomato, spring onions, noodles, fish sauce, oyster sauce and sugar and stir-fry for a further 1 minute. If the mixture looks as if it might burn, add a little water. Serve immediately.

Above: Prawns with cellophane noodles
Below: Sea bream with Thai basil

Oranges in liqueur

SOM LOY GAO

Easy to make

Serves 4
4 large oranges
115 g/4 oz soft brown sugar
500 ml/17 fl oz water
120 ml/8 fl oz orange liqueur

Approximately per portion:
870 kj/210 kcal
1 g protein
0 g fat
46 g carbohydrate

- Approximate preparation
  time: 30 minutes
- Macerating time: 12 hours

---

1. Using a sharp knife, peel the oranges and cut off the white pith. Cut the flesh crossways into slices about 1 cm/½ inch thick. Remove any pips. Arrange in a shallow dish and set aside.

2. Put the sugar and water in a pan over a medium heat and bring to the boil stirring. When the sugar has dissolved completely, lower the heat and simmer for about 20 minutes, until a thick syrup forms. Remove from the heat and set aside to cool.

3. When cold, pour the sugar syrup over the oranges and add the liqueur. set aside in the refrigerator to macerate for at least 12 hours. Before serving add some more orange liqueur, if liked.

Tip

A creamy orange ice cream would be the perfect accompaniment for this delicious tropical dish.

Melon with coconut milk

TANG THAI NAM GATI

Easy to prepare

Serves 4
1 honeydew or cantaloupe melon
400 ml/14 fl oz coconut milk
75 ml/5 tablespoons palm sugar or
  soft brown sugar
30 ml/2 tablespoons vanilla sugar
  (see Tip)

Approximately per portion:
610 kj/150 kcal
1 g protein
0 g fat
34 g carbohydrate

- Approximate preparation
  time: 1½ hours
  (1 hour cooling time)

---

1. Peel the melon, cut into quarters lengthways and remove the seeds. Then cut the quarters into bite-size pieces and chill in the refrigerator for about 1 hour.

2. Place the coconut milk, palm sugar or brown sugar and vanilla sugar in a small pan over a low heat and stir until the sugar has dissolved. Remove from the heat, set aside to cool completely, then chill in the refrigerator.

3. Transfer the melon to a serving bowl, pour over the coconut milk and serve.

Variation
You can also scoop out the melon flesh with a melon baller and reserve the half shells. Then, serve the chilled melon balls and coconut milk in melon shells on a bed of crushed ice.

Tip

To make vanilla sugar, simply store 450 g/1 lb caster sugar, together with a vanilla pod in an airtight container. The sugar will absorb the flavour of the vanilla over a few days. If you are in a hurry, use plain caster sugar and 1–2 drops vanilla essence.

Above: Oranges in liqueur
Below: Melon with coconut milk

Mango with glutinous rice

KAO NIAU MUN MANANG

Famous recipe

Serves 4
115 g/4 oz glutinous rice
200 ml/7 fl oz coconut milk
2.5 ml/½ teaspoon cornflour
salt
250 ml/8 fl oz water
45 ml/3 tablespoons sugar
2 ripe mangoes

Approximately per portion:
800 kj/190 kcal
3 g protein • 1 g fat
43 g carbohydrate

● Approximate preparation time: 40 minutes

● Soaking time: 12 hours

---

1. Rinse the rice several times in cold water. Place in a bowl, cover with cold water and set aside overnight.

2. Drain the rice and put it into a saucepan. Cover with cold water, bring to the boil, cover and simmer for 30 minutes, or until the liquid has been absorbed.

3. Heat 30 ml/2 tablespoons of the thick part of the coconut milk in a small saucepan. Stir in the cornflour, a pinch of salt and half the water. Bring to the boil, stirring. Remove from the heat and set aside.

4. Mix together the remaining coconut milk, sugar and remaining water in a saucepan over a medium heat. Bring to the boil, stirring constantly. Remove from the heat, stir in the rice and set aside.

5. Peel, stone and slice the mangoes. Divide the rice and mangoes between 4 plates. Pour over the sauce and serve.

Coconut ice cream

AISKRIM GATI

Easy to prepare

Serves 4
400 g/14 oz can coconut flesh
  in syrup
750 ml/1¼ pints coconut milk
90 g/3½ oz sugar
prepared tropical fruits, to serve

Approximately per portion:
1,900 kj/450 kcal
5 g protein
34 g fat
33 g carbohydrate

● Approximate preparation time: 20 minutes

● Freezing time: 5 hours

---

1. Drain the coconut flesh and reserve the syrup. Mix the coconut milk with the syrup and the sugar in a saucepan. Cook over a low heat, stirring constantly, for 3 minutes, but do not allow it to boil. Remove from the heat and set aside.

2. Dice the coconut flesh and stir into the coconut milk. Pour into an ice-cream maker and freeze according to the manufacturer's instructions. Alternatively, pour the mixture into a freezer-proof container and chill in the freezer. Remove from the freezer as soon as the mixture is beginning to freeze and beat vigorously with a fork to break up the ice crystals and disperse the pieces of coconut. Return to the freezer and repeat this process a second time before leaving the ice cream to freeze completely.

3. Remove the ice cream from the freezer 30 minutes before serving and transfer to the refrigerator to soften. Serve scoops of ice cream with a selection of prepared tropical fruits, if liked.

Tip

Canned coconut in syrup is available from some Chinese stores. However, you can use 400 g/14 oz fresh coconut flesh and make a syrup with 75–115 g/3–4 oz sugar and 300 ml/½ pint water. Proceed with the recipe as above.

Above: Mango with glutinous rice
Below: Coconut ice cream

Fried bananas

KLUAY TOD

Cheap and quick

Serves 4
2 large bananas
50 g/2 oz tempura flour or
    plain flour
120 ml/4 fl oz water
15 ml/1 tablespoon sugar
salt
45 ml/3 tablespoons desiccated
    coconut
15 ml/1 tablespoon sesame seeds
60 ml/4 tablespoons clear honey
vegetable oil, for deep-frying

Approximately per portion:
2,100 kj/500 kcal
3 g protein
28 g fat
60 g carbohydrate

● Approximate preparation
   time: 20 minutes

---

1. Peel the bananas, cut in half lengthways and then in half crossways. (Do not do this until you are ready to proceed or they will discolour.)

2. Beat together the flour, water, sugar and a pinch of salt to make a smooth, thick batter. Add the coconut, sesame seeds and, if necessary, 5–10 ml/1–2 teaspoons more water and mix thoroughly.

3. Heat the oil in a deep-fryer or wok. The oil is hot enough when dipping the handle of a wooden spoon into it causes small bubbles to rise. Dip the bananas in the batter and turn to coat. Fry them,

in batches if necessary, for about 2 minutes. Drain on kitchen paper and keep warm while you cook the remaining batches. Arrange the bananas on a serving dish, drizzle over the honey and serve hot.

Deep-fried pineapple rings

SAPPAROT TOD

Quick and easy to make

Serves 4
8 canned pineapple rings
90 g/3½ oz tempura flour or
    plain flour
salt
75 ml/5 tablespoons clear honey,
    plus extra for serving (optional)
15 ml/1 tablespoon lemon juice
vegetable oil, for deep-frying

Approximately per portion:
2,100 kj/500 kcal
3 g protein
28 g fat
60 g carbohydrate

● Approximate preparation
   time: 20 minutes

---

1. Drain the pineapple rings and reserve the juice. Beat together the flour and 120 ml/4 fl oz of the pineapple juice (if necessary make up the quantity of liquid needed with water) and a pinch of salt to make a smooth, thick batter. If necessary, beat in 5–10 ml/ 1–2 teaspoons more water.

2. Mix together the honey and lemon juice.

3. Heat the oil in a deep-fryer or wok. The oil is hot enough when dipping the handle of a wooden spoon into it causes little bubbles to rise. Dip the pineapple rings in the batter and turn to coat. Fry for about 2 minutes until puffed up and golden brown.

4. Drain the pineapple rings on kitchen paper. Serve hot with extra honey, if liked.

Variation
Instead of pineapple, you can use peeled and cored apples cut into fairly thick slices.

Above: Fried bananas
Below: Deep-fried pineapple rings

Great Little Cook Books

Thai Cooking

Published originally under the title
Thaiädisch kochen by Gräfe und
Unzer Verlag GmbH, München

© 1994 by Gräfe und Unzer Verlag
GmbH, München

English-language edition
© 1998 by Transedition Limited,
Oxford, England

This edition published in 2002
by Advanced Marketing,
Bicester, Oxfordshire.

Translation:
Translate-A-Book, Oxford

Editing:
Linda Doeser

Typesetting:
Organ Graphic, Abingdon

10 9 8 7 6 5 4
Printed in Dubai

ISBN 1 901683 26 5

Note:
Quantities for all recipes are given
in both metric and imperial
measures and, if appropriate, in
standard measuring spoons. They
are not interchangeable, so readers
should follow one set or the other.
5 ml = 1 teaspoon
15 ml = 1 tablespoon

Thidavadee Camsong
was born in Ratchaburi, Thailand,
in 1963 and after leaving school
she studied at the Siam
Commerce School in Bangkok. At
the same time, she learned all
about traditional Thai cuisine at
her mother's restaurant. After
leaving university, she worked as
sales manager in a Bangkok travel
agency. Since her marriage to a
German in 1989 she has been
living in Germany. She teaches
courses in Thai cuisine at an adult
education college. She also finds
time to play classical music on the
Khim and plays at Thai festivals.

Odette Teubner
was trained by her father, the
internationally renowned
photographer Christian Teubner.
Today she works exclusively in the
Teubner Studio for Food
Photography. In her free time she
is an enthusiastic painter of
children's portraits, using her own
son as a model.

Dorothee Gödert
first worked in the areas of still life
and interior photography, after
completing her training. Following
a visit to Princeton in the United
States, she started to specialize in
food photography and has worked
for a number of famous food
photographers. Since April 1988
she has been working in the
Teubner studio.